zoom

español 1

Foundation Workbook

Vincent Everett

OxBox

OXFORD

OXFORD
UNIVERSITY PRESS

Great Clarendon Street, Oxford OX2 6DP

Oxford University Press is a department of the University of Oxford.

It furthers the University's objective of excellence in research, scholarship,
and education by publishing worldwide in
Oxford New York Auckland Cape Town Dar es Salaam Hong Kong Karachi
Kuala Lumpur Madrid Melbourne Mexico City Nairobi New Delhi Shanghai
Taipei Toronto

With offices in
Argentina Austria Brazil Chile Czech Republic France Greece Guatemala
Hungary Italy Japan South Korea Poland Portugal Singapore Switzerland
Thailand Turkey Ukraine Vietnam

British Library Cataloguing in Publication Data

Data available

ISBN 978 019 912755 9

15

Printed in Great Britain by Ashford Colour Press Ltd, Gosport

Paper used in the production of this book is a natural, recyclable product made
from wood grown in sustainable forests. The manufacturing process conforms
to the environmental regulations of the country of origin.

Acknowledgements

The Publisher and authors would like to thank the following for their permission
to reproduce photographs and other copyright material:

Cover: Oxford Designers & Illustrators

P46: Brendan Howard/Shutterstock.

Illustrations by: Adrian Barclay, Stefan Chabluk. Theresa Tibbetts, James Stayte.

Audio recordings: Colette Thomson for Footstep Production; Andrew Garratt
(Engineer).

Tabla de materias

Pronunciation

Vowels

1 🎧 **Listen and practise the vowels with the actions.**

2 🎧 **Practise saying the names of these Spanish football clubs. Listen and check.**

> Gran Canaria   Salamanca   La Palma   Osasuna

3 🎧 **Try these combinations of vowels. Say them separately, then together, then in a word. Listen and check.**

> | | | |
> |---|---|---|
> | u – a | ua | cuatro |
> | e – i | ei | seis |
> | i – e | ie | siete |
> | u – e | ue | nueve |

4 **Now try saying these Spanish football clubs.**

> Real Oviedo   Bilbao   Santiago   Huelva

5 **Remember to pronounce all the vowels. Say these words.**

> siete   nueve   once   doce   quince

6 **Say these Spanish football clubs.**

> Levante   Tenerife   Elche

Pronunciation

Soft and hard consonants

1 🎧 **Listen and repeat these words. Underline the soft c (pronounced like a 'th').**

> casa   cinco   cocina

2 🎧 **Listen and repeat these words. Underline the soft g / j (pronounced like 'ch' in 'loch').**

> geografía   Los Ángeles   José

3 🎧 **Find the soft ci / ce / z sound and underline it in these Spanish football clubs. Say the words, then listen and check.**

> Barcelona   Albacete   Celta de Vigo   Zaragoza

4 🎧 **Find the soft ge / gi / j sound and underline it in these Spanish football clubs. Say the words, then listen and check.**

> Gijón   Getafe   Ejido

5 **Use everything you've learned so far. Underline the tricky bits in these names, then try saying them.**

> Badajoz   Jerez   Real Murcia   Córdoba   Numancia de Soria

Pronunciation

Spanish consonants

1 🎧 Listen, then practise saying these sounds. First on their own, then in words.

qu	qu	¿qué?
ll	ll	me llamo
rr	rr	burro
ch	ch	ocho
ñ	ñ	España

2 In *er*, *ir* and *ar*, do not change the sound of the vowel from 'e', 'i' or 'a'. Try saying these words.

> verde   número   ir al baño   escuchar

3 Underline the tricky consonants, then try saying the names of these Spanish football clubs.

Valladolid	**Deportivo La Coruña**	**Español**
Mallorca	**Valencia** **Villarreal**	**Sevilla**
Atlético Madrid	**Mallorca**	**Real Sociedad**
Santander	**Almería**	**Tenerife**

4 Pretend to read the Spanish football results. You will need the following numbers.

> cero = 0   uno = 1   dos = 2   tres = 3
> cuatro = 4   cinco = 5   seis = 6   diez = 10

Pronunciation

Words and sentences

1 🎧 Listen to these words ending in a vowel, 's' or 'n'. Circle the syllable that has the stress.

> casa   casas   casan
>
> habla   hablas   hablan

2 🎧 Listen to these words ending in a consonant (not 's' or 'n'). Circle the syllable that has the stress.

> hotel   hablar   profesor
>
> Madrid   diez

3 🎧 Listen to these words which have an accent. Circle the syllable that has the stress.

> jardín   matemáticas
>
> Almería   Los Ángeles

4 🎧 Listen and repeat. Notice how one word can run into the next.

> ¿Dónde está?
> Está en España.
> Se llama Alberto.

5 🎧 Be careful with words that look similar to English words. Say these words. Then listen and check.

> hotel   restaurante   tomate   David Beckham

6 Read these sentences aloud.

> Prefiero la comida italiana porque es deliciosa.
> Mi plato favorito es la lasaña.
> En un restaurante, como pasta y un helado de chocolate.

0.1 Quiz

1 Practise writing the Spanish characters. First trace the letter, then write it for yourself.

ñ ____ ____   í ____ ____

¿ ____ ____   á ____ ____

é ____ ____   ó ____ ____

í ____ ____   ú ____ ____

2 Now practise writing out these sentences.

a ¿Cómo te llamas? _____

b ¡Hola! Me llamo José María. _____

c ¿Y tú? _____

d Me llamo Iñigo. _____

3 🎧 Listen and identify the celebrities in the correct order.

Fernando ☐   Cesc ☐   Shakira ☐   Penélope ☐

4 Practise this dialogue for each of the celebrities.

A	B
– Hola.	– Hola.
– ¿Qué tal?	– Bien, gracias.
– ¿Cómo te llamas?	– Me llamo …

1 🎧 Javier is planning a surprise party for his little brother. To keep it secret he spells out the important words. Listen and tick the ones he mentions.

fiesta ☐   amigos ☐   helado ☐   hamburguesa ☐

iPod ☐   música ☐   osito ☐

2 🎧 Now spell out the other surprises. Listen and check.

> helado   iPod   osito

3 Read and decode the words below.

tres	cuatro	cinco	seis	siete	ocho	nueve
t	o	r	m	a	e	i

a 6óv9l *Ejemplo :* <u>móvil</u>

b 58v9s37 _____

c 58g7l4 _____

d 64d7 _____

e 67sc437 _____

f n757nj7 _____

g s89s _____

h s98t8 _____

4 Colour all the masculine nouns in red and all the feminine ones in blue.

> un amigo
> un regalo   una hamburguesa
> una fiesta   un helado   una naranja
> un deporte   la música   un grupo

0.3 La familia

1 **Complete the grid.**

Masculine	Feminine
hermano	
	tía
padre	
	madrastra
abuelo	
	prima

2 **Read and name the people in the picture.**

_____ _____ _____ _____ _____

Me llamo Ana María. Tengo un hermano.

Soy el hermano de Ana María. Me llamo Javier. Mi madre se llama Violeta.

Me llamo Violeta. Soy la madre de Ana María y Javier. Mi marido se llama Juan Carlos.

Soy Juan Carlos. Mi madre se llama Ernestina.

Soy la abuela de Javier y Ana María. Me llamo Ernestina.

3 **Point to each person in this picture and give as much information as you can about them.**

Soy ...   Tengo ...   Me llamo ...

Marco   Elena   Paz   José   Ricardo

1 Put these animals in order according to their lifespan.

Tigre: veintidós años
Serpiente: veintitrés años
Rinoceronte: cuarenta años
Cocodrilo: cuarenta y cinco años
Hipopótamo: treinta y nueve años
Elefante: setenta años
Koala: ocho años
Canguro: nueve años

45	
	Hipopótamo
22	
9	Canguro
8	

2 Draw lines to match up the answers to the questions.

a	¿Qué tal?	Me llamo Stacey.
b	¿Cómo te llamas?	Muy bien, gracias.
c	¿Cuántos años tienes?	Tengo una hermana.
d	¿Tienes hermanos?	Tengo una abuela y dos abuelos.
e	¿Tienes abuelos?	Tengo doce años.

3 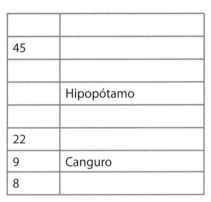 Listen and answer the questions for Stacey. Try not to get caught out.

4 Now write your own answers to the questions.

_____

_____

_____

_____

_____

1 Follow the word snake round the grid to read the conversation.
The snake can go up, down or across, but not diagonally.

Q	u	é	a	m	l	l
l	a	t	l	a	e	a
m	t	e	l	s	m	m
u	o	m	ó	c	b	o
y	b	i	e	n	e	n

2 Now try this one.

T	e	n	g	a	n	s	t
a	n	u	o	a	a	e	í
h	n	a	a	m	y	r	o
e	a	s	l	e	t	t	s
r	m	e	l	n	g	o	

3 Now create your own word snake grid using Spanish you know.

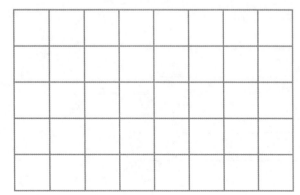

Recuerdo

In Spanish, all nouns are either masculine or feminine:
un hermano
una hermana

1 **Circle all the nouns.**

una fiesta	tres	las naranjas
a party	*three*	*the oranges*
tengo	la música	los helados
I have	*the music*	*the ice creams*
un hermano	y	
a brother	*and*	

'I can only feel nouns in here!'

2 **How did you decide what was a noun?**
Put these reasons in order of importance, 1–3.

Because of the word in front ☐

Because of the meaning ☐

Because the word looked like a noun ☐

3 **Sort these nouns into masculine and feminine by writing *un* or *una* in front of them.**

_____ hermano   _____ regalo   _____ abuelo

_____ hermana   _____ hamburguesa   _____ familia

_____ osito   _____ helado   _____ guitarra

4 **A or the? Complete the English translations.**

*Ejemplo: una fiesta : _a party_*

a un regalo: _____ present   **d** una revista: _____ magazine

b el abuelo: _____ grandfather   **e** un amigo: _____ friend

c la guitarra: _____ guitar

1 Look at the two different vocabulary pages below.
Decide who (Alex or Jordan) has …

… recorded *un/una* with nouns	Alex / Jordan
… organised their words	Alex / Jordan
… given verbs in the infinitive form	Alex / Jordan
… kept Spanish and English clear	Alex / Jordan
… shown how words can change their endings	Alex / Jordan
… highlighted tricky areas	Alex / Jordan
… shown how words fit together in phrases	Alex / Jordan

grandad un abuelo
tengo I have
dos hermanos two brothers
a mother una madre
a gran una abuela
años years

Alex

abuelo/a – grandfather/mother
hermano/a – brother/sister
madre – mother
tener – to have
    tengo – I have
    tengo un hermano
    tengo doce años – I am twelve

Jordan

2 What two things do you like about the way Alex has set out the vocabulary? And two things for Jordan?

_____

_____

_____

_____

3 Record Alex and Jordan's vocabulary in the best possible way.

¡Hola!	**Hello!**
Saludos	Greetings
¡Hola!	Hello!
Adiós	Goodbye
Hasta luego	See you later
Hasta pronto	See you soon
Soy Ana	I am Ana
Me llamo Federico	My name is Federico

Durante la clase	**In class**
escucha	listen
repite	repeat
habla	speak
lee	read
escribe	write
pregunta	ask
indica	point to
contesta	answer
mira	look
empareja	match

Quiz	**Quiz**
¿Cómo te llamas?	What's your name?
Se llama Olivia	Her name is Olivia
¿Qué tal?	How are you?
Buenos días	Good morning
Buenas tardes	Good afternoon
Buenas noches	Good night

Me flipa; me molan	**I love it; I'm into them**
uno	one
dos	two
tres	three
cuatro	four
cinco	five
seis	six
siete	seven
ocho	eight
nueve	nine
diez	ten
once	eleven
doce	twelve
trece	thirteen
catorce	fourteen
quince	fifteen
dieciséis	sixteen
diecisiete	seventeen
dieciocho	eighteen
diecinueve	nineteen
veinte	twenty

La familia	**The family**
el abuelo	grandfather
la abuela	grandmother
los abuelos	grandparents
mi padre	my father
mi madre	my mother
mis padres	my parents
el hermano	brother
la hermana	sister
el tío	uncle
la tía	aunt
el primo	cousin (m)
la prima	cousin (f)
el hermanastro	stepbrother
la hermanastra	stepsister
el padrastro	stepfather
la madrastra	stepmother
Soy hijo único	I'm an only child (m)
Soy hija única	I'm an only child (f)

¿Cuántos años tienes?	**How old are you?**
Tengo X años	I'm X years old
treinta	thirty
cuarenta	forty
cincuenta	fifty
sesenta	sixty
setenta	seventy
ochenta	eighty
noventa	ninety
cien	a hundred

Gente y números	**People and numbers**
hay	there is, there are
no hay	there isn't, there aren't

Checklist

How well do you think you can do the following? Write a sentence for each one if you can.	I can do this well	I can do this but not very well	I can't do this yet
1. Spell out loud			
2. Count to 20			
3. Say the 10s up to 100			
4. Use un/una/el/la			
5. Talk about family members			
6. Say how old I am			
7. Record vocabulary			

1A.1 Cumpleaños y fiestas

1 🎧 Play *Bópelo*. Listen and bop the words on the page as you hear them.

(lunes)   (martes)   (miércoles)   (jueves)

(viernes)   (sábado)   (domingo)

2 🎧 Read the dates of these people's birthdays. Then listen, and when you hear one of the dates, shout '*Feliz Cumpleaños*' and the person's name.

Shakira
2 de febrero

Fernando Torres
20 de marzo

Cesc Fàbregas
4 de mayo

Madonna
16 de agosto

Rio Ferdinand
7 de noviembre

Cristina Aguilera
18 de diciembre

3 Write a sentence in Spanish saying when each celebrity's birthday is.

Ejemplo: *El cumpleaños de Shakira es el dos de febrero.*

_____

_____

_____

_____

1A.2 Mis mascotas

1 🎧 **Listen to the English and Spanish ways of describing things, and try to tick which animal is being talked about.**

perro ☐

gato ☐

pez ☐

pájaro ☐

ratón ☐

tortuga ☐

> **Recuerdo**
>
> Spanish word order means that you are told what something <u>is</u> BEFORE it is described: *un gato negro*
>
> English word order describes the thing before you even know what it is: *a black … cat*

2 **Read and underline all the pets, colours and numbers.**

> Tengo una tortuga, dos perros marrones, y un gato que se llama Binki.

Álvaro

> Tenemos dos perros negros y un pez.

Elena

> Tenemos un gato blanco que se llama Chispa, y un perro marrón.

Beto

> Tengo dos animales. Un gato negro y un conejo blanco.

Nacho

> Tengo un pájaro, un ratón y un pez. El pájaro es verde, el ratón es gris, y el pez es rojo.

Paz

3 **Read again. Who has …**

a … a cat and a rabbit? _____

b … a grey mouse? _____

c … two brown dogs? _____

d … four pets? _____

e … a white cat? _____

4 **Choose two of the people from Activity 2. Draw and label their pets.**

1A.3 Lenguas y nacionalidades

soy …

inglés / inglesa
escocés / escocesa
irlandés / irlandesa
galés / galesa
portugués / portuguesa
italiano / italiana
español / española

hablo …
aprendo …

inglés
galés
portugués
italiano
español
francés

vivo en …

Inglaterra
Gales
Escocia
Portugal
Italia
España

1 Listen and tick the words in the clouds as you hear them.

2 Use the clouds to introduce each of these people.

Nombre: *Albanella*
Nacionalidad: *italiana*
Idiomas: *italiano, inglés*
Residencia: *Escocia*

Nombre: *Rachel*
Nacionalidad: *inglesa*
Idiomas: *inglés, francés*
Residencia: *Inglaterra*

Nombre: *Vanessa*
Nacionalidad: *portuguesa*
Idiomas: *inglés, portugués,*
francés
Residencia: *Inglaterra*

3 Write your own answers to these questions.

a ¿Cuál es tu nacionalidad? _____

b ¿Qué idiomas hablas? _____

c ¿Qué idiomas aprendes en el instituto? _____

d ¿Dónde vives? _____

1 🎧 **Listen to the descriptions of agents X, Y, Z and 0. Write the correct letter under each picture.**

2 **Read, and draw the disguise on each agent.**

Agente X
Tiene una barba blanca y larga.

Agente Y
Tiene un bigote negro.

Agente Z
Lleva gafas.

Agente 0
Tiene una barba negra, un bigote y pecas.
Lleva una peluca larga y rubia, y gafas.

> **rubio** – *blond*
> **castaño**– *brown*
> **una peluca** – *a wig*

| gafas | bigote | barba | pecas | peluca |

3 🎧 **Listen. Which agent has been caught?**

_____

4 **Draw and label in Spanish a picture of yourself before and after a disguise.**

1 **Draw lines to match up the name of the country with the nationality.**

Méjico	argentino
Argentina	mejicano
Colombia	colombiano
Perú	venezolano
Venezuela	peruano
Guatemala	guatemalteco
Honduras	chileno
Chile	hondureño

2 🎧 **Listen and fill in the grid.**

Name	Nationality	Lives in	Language(s)
Igor			
Marta			
Carlos			
Claudia			

3 🎧 **In Latin America, a 'z' or soft 'c' are pronounced like an 's'. In Spain, they are pronounced like an English 'th'. Read and listen to these sentences. Which is spoken in European Spanish, and which is American Spanish? Try saying them both ways.**

1 Me llamo Azucena y soy venezolana. Vivo en Venezuela.

2 Me llamo Cecilia y vivo en Cádiz, una ciudad española.

Recuerdo

In Spanish, verbs change their ending depending on the person doing the action of the verb.

1 Put the verbs into the correct columns.

ar	er	ir

visitar – *to visit*   leer – *to read*   escribir – *to write*

vivir – *to live*   hablar – *to talk*   beber – *to drink*

2 Put the persons of the verb onto the grid in the correct order.

I   we   they   he/she/it   you (plural)   you (singular)

Singular		Plural	
1st person		1st person	
2nd person		2nd person	
3rd person		3rd person	

3 🎧 Listen and follow the instructions.

4 Draw lines to match up.

a Hablamos español.   They are visiting the family.
b Visitan a la familia.   I speak English.
c Hablo inglés.   We are visiting my grandmother.
d Visitamos a mi abuela.   We speak Spanish.

1 Be the teacher. Elena has had some problems with getting capital letters right. Get out your red pen and correct her work.

> Me llamo Elena. Vivo en españa y soy Española. Hablo español y Francés. En el instituto tengo francés los Jueves y martes.

2 Read Ryan's Spanish work. He has written a long list of pets. Can you rewrite it with connectives to make it a better piece of work?

> Tengo un gato y se llama Fernando y un perro y un pájaro y no tengo conejos, y mi hermano tiene un conejo y se llama Steven (el conejo, no mi hermano).

_____

_____

_____

> pero – *but*   que – *who/which*   también – *also*
>
> aunque – *although*   sin embargo – *however*

3 Look at the pictures. Choose the best quantifier to complete each sentence.

1    2    3

1 El perro es _____ grande.

2 El pájaro es _____ inteligente.

3 El gato es _____ pequeño.

> bastante – *quite*   un poco – *a bit*   muy – *very*   demasiado – *too*

Cumpleaños y fiestas	Birthdays and festivals
enero	January
febrero	February
marzo	March
abril	April
mayo	May
junio	June
julio	July
agosto	August
septiembre	September
octubre	October
noviembre	November
diciembre	December
lunes	Monday
martes	Tuesday
miércoles	Wednesday
jueves	Thursday
viernes	Friday
sábado	Saturday
domingo	Sunday

Mis mascotas	My pets
un ratón	a mouse
un pájaro	a bird
un gato	a cat
una rata	a rat
una tortuga	a turtle / tortoise
un perro	a dog
una araña	a spider
un pez	a fish
un conejo	a rabbit
un caballo	a horse
una cobaya	a guinea pig
una serpiente	a snake
blanco/a	white
negro/a	black
rojo/a	red
azul / verde	blue / green
amarillo/a	yellow
naranja / gris	orange / grey
marrón / rosa	brown / pink
morado/a	purple

Lenguas y nacionalidades	Languages and nationalities
inglés / inglesa	English
escocés / escocesa	Scottish
irlandés / irlandesa	Irish
galés / galesa	Welsh
francés / francesa	French
español(a)	Spanish
portugués / portuguesa	Portuguese
italiano/a	Italian

¿Cómo eres?	What are you like?
Tengo …	I have …

el pelo	hair
largo / corto	long / short
liso / rizado	straight / curly
ondulado	wavy
de punta	spiky
los ojos	eyes
bigote / barba	moustache / beard
pecas	freckles
Llevo gafas	I wear glasses
Soy …	I am …
alto/a	tall
bajo/a	short
delgado/a	slim
gordo/a	fat
de talla mediana	medium size
(des)ordenado/a	(un)tidy
simpático/a	friendly
antipático/a	unfriendly
(im)paciente	(im)patient
estudioso/a	studious
perezoso/a	lazy
testarudo/a	stubborn
extrovertido/a	outgoing
tímido/a	shy
inteligente	intelligent
bobo/a	silly
(in)maduro/a	(im)mature

Checklist

How well do you think you can do the following? Write a sentence for each one if you can.	I can do this well	I can do this but not very well	I can't do this yet
1. Say dates and birthdays			
2. Talk about pets and what colour they are			
3. Make adjectives agree			
4. Give your nationality and what languages you speak			
5. Change verb endings			
6. Describe yourself			
7. Improve work with connectives and quantifiers			

1B.1 Mis asignaturas

1 🎧 **Listen to the pronunciation on the CD, then read these words aloud.**

a Words with accents:

> el ingl**é**s   la geograf**í**a   las matem**á**ticas   la inform**á**tica   la tecnolog**í**a

b Words with Spanish sounds:

> las **ci**en**ci**as   el espa**ñ**ol   la tecnolog**í**a   la **ge**ograf**í**a   la **h**istoria

2 **Masculine, feminine, singular, plural. Put the words below into the chart in the 'Asignaturas' column.**

	Asignaturas		Adjetivos	
EL	*inglés*	ES	*interesante* *difícil* *útil*	*divertido* *aburrido* *fácil*
LA	*historia*		*interesante* *difícil* *útil*	*divertida* *aburrida* *fácil*
LAS	*ciencias*	SON	*interesantes* *difíciles* *útiles*	*divertidas* *aburridas* *fáciles*

> inglés   español   dibujo   deporte   historia   música
> geografía   informática   tecnología   matemáticas   ciencias

3 **Use the chart in Activity 2 to read aloud different opinions on school subjects. How many can you do in one minute?**

Ejemplo: La historia es divertida …

4 **Use the chart again to help you complete these sentences.**

a Me gusta el _____ porque es _____ .

b Me gusta la _____ porque es _____ .

c Me gustan las _____ porque son _____ .

d Me gusta _____ .

e Me gustan _____ .

1 **Complete with the correct times.**

Ejemplo: Son las cuatro.

Son las _____ .

Son _____ _____ .

_____ _____ _____ .

Son las cinco y cuarto.

Son las dos _____ _____ .

Son las _____ y _____ .

Son _____ _____ _____ _____ .

Son las dos y media.

Son las tres y _____ .

Son las _____ y _____ .

_____ _____ _____ _____ .

Son las cinco menos cuarto.

Son las tres _____ cuarto.

Son las ocho _____ _____ .

Son las _____ _____ .

2 **Read and underline the times and the lessons. Then fill in the timetable.**

A las nueve, tengo inglés. Tengo matemáticas a las diez menos cuarto. A las once tengo geografía y a las doce menos cuarto tengo historia. A la una y cuarto tengo ciencias. Tengo música a las tres menos cuarto.

9.00	inglés
9.45	
11.00	
11.45	
1.15	
2.45	

1 🎧 **Listen. True (T) or false (F)?**

a Mi instituto es antiguo. ☐

b El patio es pequeño. ☐

c Tenemos un aula especial para tecnología. ☐

d Hay tres oficinas. ☐

e La oficina del director es grande. ☐

f Me gusta el instituto. ☐

g No hay un gimnasio. ☐

h Estudio en la biblioteca. ☐

i Como en el comedor. ☐

2 **Circle the option that best describes your own school.**

a Mi instituto es <u>moderno</u> / <u>antiguo</u>.

b El patio es <u>grande</u> / <u>pequeño</u>.

c Tenemos un aula especial para <u>informática</u> / <u>tecnología</u>.

d Hay <u>tres</u> / <u>cuatro</u> oficinas.

e La oficina <u>del director</u> / <u>de la directora</u> es grande.

f <u>Me gusta</u> / <u>No me gusta</u> el instituto.

g <u>Hay</u> / <u>No hay</u> un gimnasio.

h Estudio en <u>la biblioteca</u> / <u>el laboratorio</u>.

i Como en <u>el patio</u> / <u>el comedor</u>.

3 **Draw a plan of your school and label it in Spanish.**

1 **Carry out an experiment to evaluate different ways of learning clothes vocabulary.**

a Learn these words by writing out the words eight times each. Try not to look at the word while you write. Check your spelling afterwards.

> un jersey – *jumper*   una corbata – *tie*   una falda – *skirt*

b Learn these words by recording them in Spanish and English on your phone, mp3 player or computer.

> un vestido – *dress*   una camisa – *shirt*   unos vaqueros – *jeans*

c Learn these words by making a set of cards with words and pictures and testing yourself.

> unos zapatos – *shoes*   unos pantalones – *trousers*   una gorra – *hat*

d Learn these words by teaching them to a friend.

> unos calcetines – *socks*   una sudadera – *sweatshirt*   una chaqueta – *jacket*

2 🎧 **When you have had time to learn all the words, do the test on the CD. Listen to the words and write them in English. Record your score for each set of words.**

a

Score: ☐

b

Score: ☐

c
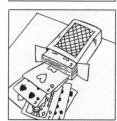
Score: ☐

d

Score: ☐

3 🎧 **Use the technique that worked best for you to learn all the words on this page. Test yourself again with the CD.**

Score: ☐

1 Put these expressions into the correct column of the table.

> es difícil   me fascina   me interesa   es aburrido/a   es interesante
> me gusta   soy fuerte en …   saco buenas notas   es fácil
> voy mal en …   me encanta   saco malas notas   el profesor es simpático

Positive	Negative

2 🎧 Listen to Pilar. Complete the grid with ☺ or ☹.

la historia	
la geografía	
el inglés	
la música	
la educación física	

3 Give your own opinions of these subjects.

el español _____

el inglés _____

la música _____

la historia _____

la geografía _____

1 **Complete each sentence with the correct adjective.**

a La historia es _____.

b Las matemáticas son _____.

c El inglés es _____.

d Los profesores son _____.

divertidos   divertido   divertida   divertidas

2 **Translate into English.**

a Comemos en el comedor. _____

b El director come en su oficina. _____

c No llevo uniforme. _____

d Hablo con mis amigos. _____

e ¿Estudias español? _____

f Mis abuelos viven en España. _____

comer – *to eat*   llevar – *to wear*   hablar – *to talk*
estudiar – *to study*   vivir – *to live*

3 **Use the words from Activity 2 to write about your own school.**

_____

_____

_____

_____

1 Which are English and which are Spanish? Highlight the Spanish words.

tecnología	technology
geography	geografía
mathematics	matemáticas
history	historia
música	music
science	ciencias

He has a very good Spanish accent.

2 Copy out the Spanish words from Activity 1. Write two important things to remember about how to spell each one.

Ejemplo: tecnología. **1** *There is no 'h'.* **2** *There is an accent on the 'ía'.*

_____

_____

_____

_____

_____

3 A cognate is a word you can re<u>cogn</u>ise from a language you already know. How many of these words are cognates? Tick the ones that are.

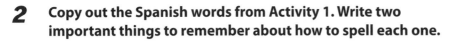

aula ☐	laboratorio ☐	oficina ☐	biblioteca ☐
gimnasio ☐	patio ☐	director ☐	

4 Cognates help when you see the written word, but can be tricky when you need to use them yourself. Think about the words you ticked in Activity 3 and put them into the table in the correct column.

Watch the spelling	Watch the pronunciation	Mean something slightly different

Mis asignaturas	My subjects
la educación física	PE
el español	Spanish
el inglés	English
la geografía	geography
la historia	history
la informática	ICT
la tecnología	design and technology
las ciencias	science
las matemáticas	mathematics
fácil	easy
difícil	difficult
útil	useful
aburrido/a	boring
divertido/a	fun, amusing
interesante	interesting
un poco	a little
bastante	fairly, quite
tan	so
muy	very
demasiado	too (much)
para mí	for me
pero	but
me gusta	I like
te gusta	you like
correcto	true
mentira	false

La hora y el horario	Time and timetable
Es la una	It is one o'clock.
... y cinco	... five past one
... y cuarto	... a quarter past one
... y veinte	... twenty past one
... y media	... half past one
Son las dos	It is two o'clock.
... menos veinticinco	... twenty-five to two
... menos cuarto	... a quarter to two
... menos diez	... ten to two
Es el mediodía	It is midday.
Es la medianoche	It is midnight.

Las instalaciones	School buildings
el aula	the classroom
el gimnasio	the gym
el laboratorio	the laboratory
el patio	the playground
la biblioteca	the library
la oficina (del director)	the office (headteacher's)
grande	large
pequeño/a	small
moderno/a	modern
antiguo/a	old
bonito/a	attractive
feo/a	ugly

cómodo/a	comfortable
leer un libro	to read a book
comer un bocadillo	to eat a sandwich
estudiar ciencias	to study science
charlar con amigos	to chat with friends
practicar deporte	to play sport
escribir cartas	to write letters

La ropa	Clothes
llevar	to wear
un jersey	a jersey
una camisa	a shirt
una camiseta	a blouse
una corbata	a tie
una falda	a skirt
una sudadera	a sweatshirt
unas zapatillas	trainers
unos calcetines	socks
unos pantalones	trousers
unos vaqueros	jeans
unos zapatos	shoes
incómodo/a	uncomfortable
elegante	stylish
práctico/a	practical
formal	formal
feo/a	ugly
ridículo/a	ridiculous
informal	informal

Checklist

How well do you think you can do the following? Write a sentence for each one if you can.	I can do this well	I can do this but not very well	I can't do this yet
1. Give opinions about school subjects			
2. Say what time lessons are			
3. Say what is in your school			
4. Describe your uniform			
5. Change verb endings			
6. Make adjectives agree			
7. Use cognates to get a head start			

1 **Put the weather words into the correct column.**

hace sol	llueve	hace frío	hay niebla
hace calor	nieva	hay tormenta	hace viento

hace …	hay …	

2 **Listen and tick the correct answer.**

1		☐		☐		☐
2		☐		☐		☐
3		☐		☐		☐
4		☐		☐		☐
5		☐		☐		☐

3 **Roll a dice and see how quickly you can say the correct weather.**

1 **Copy these activities in Spanish, in order of personal preference.**

jugar al ajedrez – *to play chess*   _____

tocar la guitarra – *to play the guitar*   _____

ir al cine – *to go to the cinema*   _____

montar a caballo – *to ride a horse*   _____

bailar salsa – *to dance salsa*   _____

jugar con videojuegos – *to play videogames*   _____

2 **Go down your list of activities, giving an opinion about each one in Spanish. Use these words:**

me gusta	no me gusta
me encanta	me aburre
me interesa	me fastidia

Ejemplo:

Me encanta ir al cine.

3 **Finish these sentences, saying what you do and don't like to do.**

Si hace sol … _____

_____

Si hace calor … _____

_____

Si hace frío … _____

_____

Si llueve … _____

_____

Si hay tormenta … _____

_____

1 Match up the captions to the pictures.

> me levanto   me lavo   me despierto   me ducho   me peino
> desayuno   me visto   me lavo los dientes

a

b

c

d

e

f

g

h

2 🎧 Listen to Javier playing a dice game. What has he 'forgotten' to do when he says he goes to school?

 Me lavo los dientes.

 Me visto.

 Me ducho.

 Me peino.

 Desayuno.

 Voy al colegio.

3 Now play the dice game yourself.

1 **Read the list of activities. Are they things you do after school?**
Put a tick or a cross.

	Yo	Miriam
Veo la tele – *I watch TV*	☐	☐
Paseo al perro – *I walk the dog*	☐	☐
Hago los deberes – *I do my homework*	☐	☐
Ceno – *I have dinner*	☐	☐
Meriendo – *I have tea*	☐	☐
Descanso – *I rest*	☐	☐
Salgo – *I go out*	☐	☐

2   **Listen to Miriam. Does she do the same things as you?**
Tick the boxes for her.

3 **Use your list to say what you do in the evening.**

Ejemplo:

> Por la tarde paseo al perro ...
> Por la tarde no ...

4 **Read these times and write what you are usually doing then.**

A las cuatro _____

A las cinco _____

A las seis _____

A las siete _____

A las ocho _____

A las nueve _____

A las diez _____

1 **What do you do at the weekend? Put these activities into the grid.**

> dormir hasta las diez   levantarme temprano
> visitar a mi abuela   comer en un restaurante
> hacer deporte   ver a mis amigos
> salir con mi familia

Puedo – *I can*	No puedo – *I can't*
Me fastidia – *It gets on my nerves*	Prefiero – *I prefer*

2 🎧 **Listen to Miriam. How would you describe her weekends?**

fun ☐   frustrating ☐   lazy ☐

Explain why.

_____

_____

3 **Use the grid in Activity 1 to write sentences about your own weekends.**

El fin de semana puedo …

_____

_____

_____

_____

Recuerdo

Reflexive verbs
When you look at your reflection you see … yourself.
Me lavo – I wash myself
Me visto – I dress myself

1 **Spot the odd one out. Explain why it is different.**

me ducho	me visto	desayuno	me lavo

_____

2 **Think like a Spanish person. Complete the grids.**

Ejemplo:

English	I get dressed
In betweenish	I dress myself
Spanish	Me visto

I get washed
Me lavo

I shower myself

Me despierto

I am called

3 **Draw lines to match up the Spanish and English.**

a Me despierto.   He gets up.
b Se levanta.   I wake up.
c Se visten.   Do you have a shower?
d ¿Te duchas?   They get dressed.

Recuerdo

All verbs change their endings. Some verbs also change part of their stem. These are called radical-changing verbs.

Jugar (ue)

juego	jugamos
juegas	jugáis
juega	**jue**gan

It is a good idea to note down the change like this: *Jugar (ue)*

1 **How would you write these verbs in your vocabulary list?**

Ejemplo: Jugar (ue)

preferir – prefiero, prefieres, prefiere, preferimos, preferís, prefieren _____

querer – quiero, quieres, quiere, queremos, queréis, quieren _____

poder – puedo, puedes, puede, podemos, podéis, pueden _____

2 **Give three reasons why it might be better to write *jugar (ue)* instead of writing out the whole verb.**

_____

_____

_____

3 **Translate into Spanish.**

  a I prefer _____

  b We prefer _____

  c You want _____

  d He wants _____

  e I can _____

  f We can _____

El tiempo — *The weather*

El tiempo	*The weather*
hace buen tiempo	*it's fine / it's a nice day*
hace mal tiempo	*it's bad weather / it's not a nice day*
hace sol	*it's sunny*
hace calor	*it's hot*
hace frío	*it's cold*
hace viento	*it's windy*
hay tormenta	*it's stormy*
hay niebla	*it's foggy*
hay nubes	*it's cloudy*
llueve / nieva	*it's raining / it's snowing*
la primavera	*spring*
el verano	*summer*
el otoño	*autumn*
el invierno	*winter*
jugar a/al/a la	*to play*
el fútbol	*football*
el baloncesto	*basketball*
el ciclismo	*cycling*
el atletismo	*athletics*
el boxeo	*boxing*
la pelota vasca	*pelota*
el voleibol	*volleyball*

Tiempo libre — *Free time*

Tiempo libre	*Free time*
ver la tele	*to watch TV*
salir con amigos	*to go out with friends*
tocar la guitarra	*to play the guitar*
ir al cine	*to go to the cinema*
montar a caballo	*to ride a horse*
bailar en la disco	*to dance in a disco*
jugar al ajedrez	*to play chess*
jugar con videojuegos	*to play computer games*
me apasiona	*I love*
me aburre	*it's boring*
me molesta	*it annoys me*
me fastidia	*it gets on my nerves*
navegar por internet	*to surf the net*
poder	*to be able*
preferir / prefiero	*to prefer / I prefer*
querer	*to like / want*
si	*if*
sí	*yes*

Por la mañana — *In the morning*

Por la mañana	*In the morning*
levantarse	*to get up*
lavarse	*to get washed*
me lavo (los dientes)	*I clean (my teeth)*
ducharse	*to have a shower*
cepillarse	*to brush*
me cepillo (el pelo)	*I brush my hair*
peinarse	*to comb / do hair*
ponerse	*to put on (clothes)*
desayunar	*to have breakfast*

despertarse	*to wake up*
vestirse	*to dress*
almorzar (ue)	*to have lunch*

Por la tarde — *In the afternoon*

Por la tarde	*In the afternoon*
a las trece horas	*at 13:00 hours (1 p.m.)*
descansar	*to relax*
merendar (ie)	*to have a snack*
pasear al perro	*to walk the dog*
hacer los deberes	*to do homework*
cenar	*to have supper*
acostarse (ue)	*to go to bed*
dormirse (ue)	*to fall asleep*
ir	*to go*
hacer compras	*to do the shopping*
la piscina	*swimming pool*
nadar	*to swim*

El fin de semana — *(At) the weekend*

El fin de semana	*(At) the weekend*
hasta las diez	*until ten o' clock*
tarde / temprano	*late / early*
de acuerdo	*agreed*
montar en bicicleta	*to ride a bike*
el sábado	*on Saturday*
los sábados	*on Saturdays*
la cocina	*kitchen*
las tostadas	*toast*
los cereales	*cereal*
en tren	*by train*
frente a	*opposite*
el mar	*the sea*
pasarlo bomba	*to have a great time*

Checklist

How well do you think you can do the following? Write a sentence for each one if you can.	I can do this well	I can do this but not very well	I can't do this yet
1. Talk about the weather			
2. Say what you like and don't like doing			
3. Say what you do in the morning, evening and at weekends			
4. Use radical-changing verbs			
5. Use reflexive verbs			
6. Record information on verbs			

1   **Match up the captions and the pictures.**

> el campo   la ciudad   la costa   la montaña

a    **b**    **c**    **d**

_____ ☐   _____ ☐   _____ ☐   _____ ☐

2   🎧 **Listen. Where do they live? Write the correct number in each box above.**

3   **Randomsville: Toss a coin to see what is in the town.**

Heads = *Hay* ... (there is).
Tails = *No hay* ... (there isn't).

Ejemplo: Hay un supermercado ...

un supermercado	una piscina	un hospital
un museo		un parque
un zoo	una bolera	un colegio

4   **Use these words to write sentences about Randomsville.**

Es ...   Está ...
una ciudad   grande   en la costa   en la montaña
un pueblo   pequeño   en el campo   en España

_____

_____

1 **Do the maths.**

Ejemplo: to + the = to the

a + el = _____   a + los = _____

a + la = _____   a + las = _____

> a las   a los   al   a la

2 **Use this grid to make up sentences.**

Voy	al	supermercado instituto parque	con mis amigos. con mi familia. todos los días. a menudo. a veces.
	a la	piscina bolera oficina de Correos	
	a los	grandes almacenes	
	a las	tiendas	

3 🎧 **Listen and do the actions.**

4 **Put on your favourite song. Make up 'a la izquierda' actions to go with it. Write down the instructions.**

_____

_____

_____

_____

1 **Read and underline all the names of rooms.**

> Hola, soy Carmen. Me gusta mi casa. A la izquierda hay una cocina. Enfrente de la cocina está el salón. En el centro está mi dormitorio y el dormitorio de mis padres. Mis padres tienen el dormitorio grande. Finalmente, a la derecha está el cuarto de baño.

2 **Read again, and draw in the rooms on this plan.**

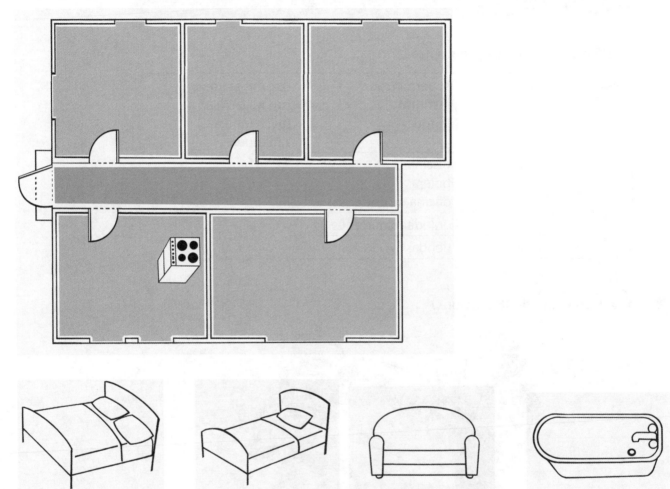

3 🎧 **Listen and add the three extra details to the plan.**

1 Use these words to label the pictures.

> estantería   armario   escritorio   libros   póster
> televisor   ordenador   ropa

Isabelle

Iñaki

Alejandro

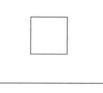

Lola

2 🎧 Listen to the four friends. Number each picture correctly.

3 Use this grid to talk about your own bedroom.

En mi dormitorio tengo …	un armario	muy	grande
	un escritorio	un poco	pequeño
En mi dormitorio hay …	un televisor	no muy	elegante
No tengo …	un ordenador	demasiado	moderno
		bastante	bonito
	una cama		grande
	una lámpara		pequeña
	una alfombra		elegante
	una silla		moderna
			bonita

1 **Find four words to describe each picture.**

a

_____

_____

_____

_____

b

_____

_____

_____

_____

c

_____

_____

_____

_____

museos – *museums*   industrial – *industrial*   granjas – *farms*
turistas – *tourists*   pintoresco – *picturesque*   tranquilo – *quiet*
animado – *busy*   gente – *people*   verde – *green*
monumentos – *monuments*   paisaje – *scenery*   tráfico – *traffic*

2 **Find the sentences in these word snake grids.**

E	d	o	c	o
s	a	y	i	
a	m	h	f	
n	i	a	á	
u	m	y	r	
c	h	o	t	

Es animado y hay mucho tráfico.

E	u	i	l	o
s	q	e	v	y
t	n	r	d	e
r	a			

_____

_____

3 **Now make up your own word snake to describe a place.**

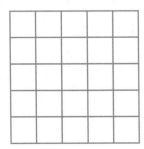

es …   hay …   con …   y …

2B.6A Labolengua

1 **Fill in the grids with the words below.**

to be (permanent quality)	ser
I am	
you are	
he/she/it is	
we are	
you are (plural)	
they are	

to be (position or temporary state)	estar
I am	
you are	
he/she/it is	
we are	
you are (plural)	
they are	

> **Recuerdo**
>
> Spanish has two verbs meaning 'to be':
> *Ser* for permanent qualities;
> *estar* for position or temporary state.

soy   estoy   estás   eres   está   es   estamos   somos
estáis   sois   son   están

2 🎧 **Listen and check. Then listen and repeat with actions.**

Ser – on each person, bang your hand on the table to show it is permanent.
Estar – on each person, wobble your hand to show it is a temporary state.

3 **Decide which group of words goes with *soy* … and which goes with *estoy* … Then write out the words in sentences.**

español(a) – *Spanish*   de Madrid – *from Madrid*
bastante inteligente – *quite intelligent*   estudiante – *a student*

en mi casa – *at home*   en la cama – *in bed*
enfermo/a – *ill*   triste – *sad*

1 Find the information in this Spanish address.

Ana García López
C/ Luís Roldán 23, 3° 2ª
50012 ZARAGOZA
(Aragón)

Her first name is _____ .

Her surnames are _____ (her father's surname)
and _____ (her mother's surname).

She lives at number _____ on _____ Street,

on the _____ floor, _____ door.

Her postcode is _____ .

The city is _____ .

The region is _____ .

2 Now write out the name and address of someone you know, using the Spanish style.

Vivo en …	I live in …
Está en …	It is in …
la montaña	the mountains
la costa	the coast
el campo	the countryside
la ciudad	the city
un pueblo	a town
una aldea	a village
un barrio	a neighbourhood
las afueras	the outskirts

¿Dónde está?	Where is it?
siempre	always
todos los días	every day
a menudo	often
a veces	sometimes
nunca	never
una vez a la semana	once a week
dos veces a la semana	twice a week
un supermercado	a supermarket
un parque	a park
una estación	a station
un banco	a bank
un museo	a museum
una catedral	a cathedral
un zoo	a zoo
un colegio	a junior school
un cine	a cinema
un parque de atracciones	a theme park
la bolera	the bowling alley
el polideportivo	the sports centre
la piscina	the swimming pool
la oficina de Correos	the post office
el ayuntamiento	the town hall
la iglesia	the church
los grandes almacenes	the department store
la parada de autobús	the bus stop
las tiendas	the shops
Sigue / Siga	Carry on
Todo recto	Straight ahead
Tuerce / Tuerza	Turn
Cruza / Cruce	Cross
Toma / Tome	Take
el puente	the bridge
la primera / segunda / tercera	the first / second / third
la calle	the street
a la derecha / izquierda	on the right / left

Mi casa	My house
un sótano	a basement
la planta baja	the ground floor
la primera planta	the first floor
el ático	the attic
una entrada	an entrance hall
las escaleras	the stairs
una cocina	a kitchen
un salón	a living room

un comedor	a dining room
un dormitorio	a bedroom
un cuarto de baño	a bathroom
una ducha	a shower
un aseo	a toilet
un despacho	an office
un jardín	a garden
un balcón	a balcony
una piscina	a swimming pool

Mi dormitorio	My bedroom
un armario	a wardrobe
una cama	a bed
un escritorio	a desk
unas estanterías	a bookcase / some shelves
una mesita de noche	a bedside table
una alfombra	a rug
una cómoda	a chest of drawers
una silla	a chair
unas cortinas	curtains
una puerta	a door
una ventana	a window
una lámpara	a lamp
delante de	in front of
enfrente de	facing
detrás de	behind
encima de	on / on top of
debajo de	under
entre	between
al lado de	next to
cerca de / lejos de	near to / far from

Checklist

How well do you think you can do the following?			
Write a sentence for each one if you can.			
	I can do this well	I can do this but not very well	I can't do this yet
1. Say where you live			
2. Talk about what there is in your town			
3. List the rooms in your house			
4. Say where the rooms are			
5. Talk about your bedroom			
6. Use ser and estar			
7. Read a Spanish address			

1 Label these pictures of things to eat in Spanish.

_____   _____   _____

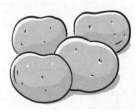

_____   _____   _____

| queso   patatas   carne   pan   pollo   chocolate |

2 Think like a Spanish person. Fill in the grids.

Ejemplo:

English	*garlic bread*
In betweenish	*bread of garlic*
Spanish	*pan de ajo*

roast chicken
chicken roast

a cheese sandwich
un bocadillo de queso

chile con carne

potatoes fried
patatas fritas

3 Write the Spanish for the following.

a ham sandwich   un _____ de _____

a chocolate cake   un _____ de _____

| jamón – *ham*   un pastel – *a cake* |

3A.2 Comida sana

comida italiana

comida malsana

comida deliciosa

comida sana

fruta

1 🎧 **Listen. For each category of food mentioned, see how many different foods you can say. Use vocabulary page 55 to help (or page 103 of the Students' Book).**

Ejemplo: Comida italiana: pizza, pasta, pan de ajo …

2 **Read the texts. Then answer the questions.**

> Lionel
> Me gusta comer postres, pero no me gusta mucho la fruta. Prefiero helados o pasteles. Contienen mucho azúcar, pero me gustan.

> Cristiano
> Me gusta la comida rápida. Me encanta comer hamburguesas, patatas fritas. Está bien, porque no como postres ni bombones.

> Magda
> Me gusta comer fruta y verduras. No como carne y no como pescado.

a Who eats fast food? _____

b Who doesn't like fruit? _____

c Who eats a lot of sweet things? _____

d Who is a vegetarian? _____

e Who doesn't eat sweet things? _____

f Who likes to eat fruit? _____

3 **Underline the sentences in Activity 2 that could also apply to you. Use them to write about yourself.**

_____

_____

_____

1 🎧 **Listen to the two people ordering food. Who do you think they are? Tick the ones you think they might be.**

an athlete ☐

a British tourist ☐

a supermodel ☐

your teacher ☐

a millionaire ☐

2 **Create a special menu (in Spanish) for each of the three other people on the list in Activity 1.**

Comida

Bebida

Comida

Bebida

Comida

Bebida

3 **Practise ordering from the menus.**

(no) tengo hambre ...   (no) tengo sed ...
¡oiga! para mí ...   quiero ...
para beber ...   para comer ...
gracias

3A.4 ¡Oiga, camarero!

1   Read these four jokes and match them up with their English translations.

1
– ¡Oiga, camarero! Hay una mosca en mi sopa.
– Lo siento, señor. ¿Es usted vegetariano?

a
– Waiter, waiter! There's a dead fly in my soup.
– Hey, sir, I'm a waiter, not a lifeguard. ☐

2
– ¡Oiga, camarero! Hay una araña en mi sopa.
– ¿Una araña? Sí, le gusta comer moscas.

b
– Waiter, waiter! There's a spider in my soup.
– A spider? Yes, he likes to eat the flies. ☐

3
– ¡Oiga, camarero! Hay un ratón en mi sopa.
– Lo siento. No tengo moscas hoy.

c
– Waiter, waiter! There's a fly in my soup.
– I'm sorry, sir. Are you a vegetarian? ☐

4
– ¡Oiga, camarero! Hay una mosca muerta en mi sopa.
– ¡Oiga, señor, soy camarero, no soy socorrista!

d
– Waiter, waiter! There's a mouse in my soup.
– I'm sorry. I don't have any flies today. ☐

2   Find the Spanish for these words in the jokes.

a fly	_____	soup	_____
a spider	_____	there is	_____
I'm sorry	_____	to eat	_____
lifeguard	_____	I don't have any	_____
today	_____	a mouse	_____

3   🎧 Listen to the jokes and underline any words you think are tricky to pronounce. Listen again and repeat these words.

4   Practise telling one of the jokes until … you can read it aloud perfectly, or … you know it off by heart. Record it on your phone or mp3, or tell it to your teacher.

1 **Read about the foods and identify what they are.**

a Se come mucho en Italia. Es deliciosa. Contiene pan, tomate, queso, jamón, aceitunas … Se come caliente y con ensalada. _____

b Se come mucho en Inglaterra. Contiene carne o verduras. Es muy picante. Se come con arroz. _____

c Se come mucho en Francia. Contiene harina, huevos y leche. Es dulce. Se come con limón y azúcar. _____

d Se come en el Japón. Contiene pescado crudo y arroz. A veces contiene algas. Es muy sano. _____

| curry | sushi | pizza | pancakes |

2 **Explain the English dish Toad in the Hole to a Spanish person.**

| se come en … | se come con … | es … | contiene … |

_____

_____

_____

| una salchicha – *sausage* | la harina – *flour* | un huevo – *egg* | leche – *milk* |

Recuerdo

In Spanish, there is a formal word for 'you'. It uses the third person instead of the second:

¿Tienes pulgas? → *¿Tiene pulgas?*
Do you have fleas? → Do you have fleas? (formal)

In English the Queen is addressed in the third person:
'Does your Majesty have …?'

1 **Highlight the difference between the formal and informal forms.**

Formal – 3rd person	Informal – 2nd person
tiene	tienes
desea	deseas

2 **Join up the pairs that mean the same thing. Circle the ones that are in the formal form.**

Aquí tiene. – *Here you are.*

¿Qué deseas? – *What would you like?*

¿Quiere …? – *Do you want …?*

¿Tienes …? – *Do you have any …?*

¿Tiene …? – *Do you have any …?*

¿Quieres …? – *Do you want …?*

Aquí tienes. – *Here you are.*

¿Qué desea? – *What would you like?*

3 🎧 **Listen. Formal or informal? Circle the correct one.**

1 Formal / Informal

2 Formal / Informal

3 Formal / Informal

1 Look at the vocabulary on page 55 (or page 103 in the Students' Book). Make yourself a memory jogging recipe by putting together ingredients that begin with the same letter of the alphabet.

Ejemplo:
atún, arroz, azúcar

un café con chocolate … y carne
_____

_____

_____   _____

_____   _____

_____   _____

Es la hora de comer / *It's time to eat*

la cena	*evening meal*
la comida	*midday meal*
la merienda	*(afternoon) snack*
a eso de	*at about*
el chocolate	*chocolate*
el pan de ajo	*garlic bread*
la carne	*meat*
las verduras	*vegetables*
los cereales	*cereal*
los churros	*churros*
un bocadillo de queso	*cheese sandwich*
un paquete de patatas fritas	*packet of crisps*
un pollo asado	*roast chicken*
una paella	*paella*
una pizza	*pizza*

Comida sana / *Healthy food*

el atún	*tuna*
los mariscos	*shellfish*
el pescado	*fish*
el salmón	*salmon*
las gambas	*prawns*
los calamares	*squid*
un melocotón	*peach*
un plátano	*banana*
una ensalada verde	*green salad*
una manzana	*apple*
una naranja	*orange*
contiene mucha grasa	*it contains a lot of fat*
contiene mucho azúcar	*it contains a lot of sugar*
es (muy) …	*it's (very)*
… sano/a	*healthy*
… malsano/a	*unhealthy*
… soso/a	*bland*
… delicioso/a	*delicious*
son (muy) …	*they are (very)*
… sanos/as	*healthy*
… malsanos/as	*unhealthy*
… sosos/as	*bland*
… deliciosos/as	*delicious*

¡Tengo hambre! / *I'm hungry!*

una coca-cola	*a coca-cola*
una fanta naranja	*fizzy orange*
un café solo	*black coffee*
un café con leche	*white coffee*
un vaso de vino tinto	*a glass of red wine*
un vaso de vino blanco	*a glass of white wine*
una cerveza	*a beer*
un agua mineral con gas	*sparkling mineral water*
un agua mineral sin gas	*still mineral water*

tengo hambre	*I'm hungry*
tengo sed	*I'm thirsty*
para comer	*to eat*
para beber	*to drink*

¡Oiga, camarero! / *Waiter!*

una cuchara	*a spoon*
un tenedor	*a fork*
un cuchillo	*a knife*
¿Dónde está …?	*Where is …?*
pedí	*I asked for*
hay	*there is*
una mosca	*a fly*
lo siento	*I'm sorry*
lo traigo	*I'll bring it*
en seguida	*at once*
traigo otro	*I'll bring another*

Me encanta la comida / *I love food*

el arroz	*rice*
la pasta	*pasta*
las especias	*spices*
es muy / es poco	*it's very / it's not very*
contiene mucho	*it contains a lot (of)*
contiene poco	*it contains little (not a lot of)*
utiliza mucho	*it uses a lot (of)*
utiliza poco	*it uses little (not a lot of)*

Checklist

How well do you think you can do the following?			
Write a sentence for each one if you can.			
	I can do this well	I can do this but not very well	I can't do this yet
1. Talk about mealtimes			
2. Talk about healthy food			
3. Say what you like to eat			
4. Order food in a café			
5. Complain in a café			
6. Describe food from different countries			
7. Create memory joggers			

1　Write the correct word(s) under each picture.

a

b

c

d

e

Ejemplo: coche

f

g

h

i

autobús　metro　barco　bicicleta　tren　avión　coche　autocar　a pie

2　🎧 Listen for the correct form of transport for each person.

1 ☐　4 ☐

2 ☐　5 ☐

3 ☐　6 ☐

3　Draw lines to link up the parts of the sentences so they all make sense.

a　Voy al instituto　　en tren　　porque es más barato.

b　Voy a Orlando　　a pie　　porque es más corto.

c　Voy a Londres　　en avión　　porque es más cómodo.

d　Voy a mi dormitorio　　en coche　　porque es más divertido.

1 🎧 **Listen. Find the right word and say it as soon as you can.**

a un camping – *a campsite*
b un hotel – *a hotel*
c un albergue juvenil – *a youth hostel*
d una habitación – *a room*
e sábanas – *sheets*
f una pensión – *a guest house*

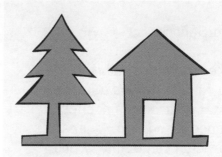

2 **Read the adverts and underline the Spanish for the following words. Decide what is being described in each (a–f).**

beach showers balcony basic restaurant young people
double bed cheap pool rooms

① Cinco estrellas, restaurante, piscina, canchas de tenis, 530 habitaciones. ☐

② Está cerca de la playa. Duchas, piscina, parking para coches, sitio para tiendas o caravanas. ☐

③ Tiene balcón, cuarto de baño con ducha, una cama doble y vistas al mar. Hay un televisor y un minibar. ☐

④ Es barato y básico, perfecto para jóvenes que quieren explorar el campo. ☐

3 **Write a sentence about where you are going to stay on holiday.**

Ejemplo: Voy a [una pensión] porque está cerca del mar, pero es muy barata.

_____

_____

voy a … – *I'm going to*   hay … – *there is*   tiene … – *it has*
es … – *it is*   está … – *it is (position)*

1 Read the letter and fill in the details next to it.

Estimado Señor,

Quiero reservar dos habitaciones para una familia de dos adultos y dos niños. Es para tres noches, del ocho al once de agosto. Queremos una habitación con ducha, y una con baño para los niños. Los niños tienen seis y ocho años. Nos gustaría tener un televisor y WiFi en la habitación. Vamos a comer en el restaurante del hotel, y somos vegetarianos.

Atentamente,

Dates: _____

Number of rooms: _____

Number of people: _____

Bathroom: _____

Room facilities: _____

Important note: _____

2 Write a similar letter for this family.

4-9 julio

Estimado Señor,

_____

_____

_____

_____

_____

Atentamente,

1 **Try to match up the sentence halves.**

1 Voy a ir a ☐   a una tienda.

2 Voy a trabajar en ☐   b la piscina.

3 Voy a alojarme en ☐   c un hotel.

4 Voy a nadar en ☐   d museos.

5 Voy a visitar ☐   e España.

2 🎧 **Listen and check.**

3 **Read the information below. Which sentence tells you …?**
Give an answer for each.

where the museum is	Ejemplo: ☐ b	*in Figueres*
when it is open in the summer	☐	_____
when it is open the rest of the year	☐	_____
what days it is shut	☐	_____
who gets free entry / discounts	☐	_____
how long it takes to walk from the station	☐	_____
who Dalí was	☐	_____
how far it is from Barcelona	☐	_____
how to get there from Barcelona and how long it takes	☐	_____

a Dalí fue un pintor español muy famoso.

b El Museo Dalí está en Figueres, al norte de Barcelona.

c En junio, julio, agosto y septiembre el museo está abierto de 9h a 20h siete días a la semana.

d De octubre a mayo está abierto de 10.30h a 18h, y está abierto de martes a domingo.

e No está abierto el 25 de diciembre y el 1 de enero.

f Los niños de 0 a 8 años entran gratis y hay descuentos para estudiantes y jubilados (de más de 60 años).

g Figueres está a 100 kilómetros de Barcelona.

h En tren o en coche, es un viaje de una hora y media.

i Si vas en tren, el museo está a 15 minutos andando de la estación de Figueres.

3B.5 Al extranjero

1 Draw lines to match up the Spanish and the English.

a ¿Adónde vas de vacaciones?   Where are you going on holiday?
b ¿Cuándo vas a ir?   How long are you going to be there?
c ¿Cuánto tiempo vas a estar allí? What are you going to do?
d ¿Cómo vas a viajar?   How are you going to travel?
e ¿Qué tiempo hace en agosto?   What is the weather like in August?
f ¿Qué vas a hacer?   When are you leaving?

2 Find these question words in Activity 1.

a where   _____

b when   _____

c how   _____

d what   _____

e how long   _____

3 🎧 Listen and note the answer to each question in Spanish.

1 _____   4 _____

2 _____   5 _____

3 _____   6 _____

4 🎧 Listen to the questions. Use your answers to Activity 3 to reply in Spanish. Then listen again and give your own answers.

What is qué?

Yes, that's right.

Recuerdo

Use 'going to' to talk about the future.
For example:

_____	Voy	a	nadar en la piscina
_____	Vas	a	salir con tus amigos
_____	Va	a	ir de vacaciones
_____	Vamos	a	comer a la una
_____	Vais	a	viajar a Colombia
_____	Van	a	jugar al baloncesto

1 Write the correct person from this list next to each verb in the examples above.

> I   we   they   he/she/it   you   you (plural)

2 Translate the examples in the *Recuerdo* box into English.

> salir – *to go out*   viajar – *to travel*   ir – *to go*   comer – *to eat*   jugar – *to play*

Ejemplo: I am going to swim in the pool. _____

_____

_____

_____

_____

_____

3 Translate into Spanish.

a I am going to eat in a restaurant. _____

b She is going to visit a museum. _____

c We are going to travel by plane. _____

d They are going to work in a café. _____

1 🎧 **Listen and tick off any words in the boxes that you hear.**

me gusta – *I like*	puedo – *I can*
me encanta – *I love*	voy a – *I'm going to*
quiero – *I want*	prefiero – *I prefer*
me gustaría – *I would like*	no …

ir – *to go*	alojarme – *to stay*
visitar – *to visit*	viajar – *to travel*
ir de compras – *to go shopping*	salir – *to go out*
explorar – *to explore*	nadar – *to swim*
sacar fotos – *to take photos*	comer – *to eat*

en un restaurante – *in a restaurant*	a España – *to Spain*
en un hotel – *in a hotel*	en la piscina – *in the pool*
a la playa – *to the beach*	con mis amigos – *with my friends*
en la ciudad – *in the city*	con mi familia – *with my family*

2 **Now it's your turn. Start with *Voy a ir a España* … then roll a dice for a connective. Carry on for as long as you can.**

Voy a ir a España …

 y – *and*

 pero – *but*

 porque – *because*

 por ejemplo – *for example*

 sin embargo – *however*

 también – *also*

El transporte	Transport
en autobús (el)	by bus
en metro (el)	by underground
en barco (el)	by boat
en bicicleta (la)	by bike
en tren (el)	by train
en avión (el)	by plane
en coche (el)	by car
en autocar (el)	by coach
un viaje	a journey
viajar	to travel
cómodo/a	comfortable
barato/a	cheap
corto/a	short
divertido/a	amusing
un billete	a ticket
ida y vuelta	return
cada veinte minutos	every 20 minutes
tardar	to take time

Alojamiento	Accommodation
alojarse	to board / to stay
un albergue juvenil	youth hostel
una pensión	bed and breakfast
un camping	campsite
quedarse	to stay
vale la pena	it's worth it
antiguo/a	ancient / old
tan … como	as … as
mejor	better
el/la mejor	the best
peor	worse
el/la peor	the worst
la sábana	sheet
la habitación	room
el ascensor	lift

Quiero reservar …	I want to reserve …
reservar	to reserve / to book
una reserva	a booking
confirmar	to confirm
incluido	included
el precio	the price
cerrar	to close
cerrado/a	closed
abrir	to open
abierto/a	open
una plaza	a camping plot
una tienda	a tent
incluso	inclusive
acampar	to pitch a tent

¿Adónde vamos?	Where shall we go?
precioso/a	pretty

maravilloso/a	marvellous
cada	each / every
media hora	half hour
apreciar	to appreciate
una parada	stop (bus)
perderse	to get lost
encontrarse	to meet/find each other
el dinero	money
tener suerte	to be lucky
menores de	under the age of
la estación	station
nace	is born
se casa con	marries
un juguete	toy
inolvidable	unforgettable
divertido/a	amusing
genial	great
fatal	awful
sensacional	amazing
guay	cool
pasarlo bomba	to have a great time
un parque de atracciones	fun fair / theme park
el mercado	market
antiguo/a	ancient
un guía	a guide (person)
una guía	a guide book
orientarse	to find your way
guardar	to keep (safe)
vigilar	to look after
una torre	tower
una tumba	tomb
las normas	rules and regulations

Checklist

How well do you think you can do the following? Write a sentence for each one if you can.	I can do this well	I can do this but not very well	I can't do this yet
1. Compare forms of transport			
2. Use 'going to' to talk about the future			
3. Book holiday accommodation			
4. Talk about holiday activities			
5. Extend your answers			

1 Write the correct Spanish word or phrase under each picture.

comer	jugar	pasear	ver una película
ver el fútbol	ir de compras	nadar	

a

_____ ☐

b

_____ ☐

c

_____ ☐

d

_____ ☐

e

_____ ☐

f

_____ ☐

g

_____ ☐

2 🎧 Listen to what you can and can't do in the town. Tick or cross each picture.

3 Use your answers to Activity 2 to talk in short sentences about the town.

> Se puede …

> No se puede …

4 Write about what you can and can't do in your own town.

_____

_____

_____

_____

_____

_____

_____

4A.2 ¿Adónde fuiste?

1 🎧 **Listen and repeat.**

fui	*I went*	fuimos	*we went*
fuiste	*you went*	fuisteis	*you (plural) went*
fue	*he/she/it went*	fueron	*they went*

2 **Translate into English.**

a

Marisa fue a Argentina. _____

Fue en agosto. _____

Fue en avión. _____

Fue a visitar a su familia. _____

b

Fuimos a España. _____

Fuimos en julio. _____

Fuimos a la playa. _____

Fuimos en coche. _____

c

Mis amigos fueron a Francia. _____

Fueron en barco. _____

Fueron en abril. _____

Fueron a París. _____

Fueron de compras. _____

3 **Translate into Spanish.**

a I went to Spain. _____

b I went by plane. _____

c I went in July. _____

d I went to the beach. _____

Preterite: I swam, I ate, I decided, I went			
nad**ar**	com**er**	decid**ir**	**ir**
nad**é**	com**í**	decid**í**	**fui**

1 Read the text and underline the six preterite endings.

El año pasado fui a España. Normalmente voy a Málaga, pero decidí ir a Madrid. Normalmente voy a la playa, pero en Madrid visité galerías de arte. Comí en unos restaurantes fantásticos. Normalmente no me gusta la comida española. Cuando voy a Málaga, hablo inglés, pero en Madrid hablé español. En Málaga me alojo en un camping, sin embargo, en Madrid me alojé en un hotel de cinco estrellas.

2 Look back at Activity 1 and complete the table.

Normally	Last year
goes to Málaga	
goes to the beach	
doesn't like Spanish food	
speaks English	
camps	

3 Write about your own holidays.

Normalmente voy a _____

pero el año pasado _____.

Normalmente me alojo en _____

pero el año pasado _____.

Normalmente como _____

pero el año pasado _____.

1 Put the expressions below into the correct column in the table.

Me gustó	¡Qué …!	Fue …	_____é
Ejemplo: me gustó *= I liked it* *(it pleased me)*			

me encantó – *I loved it!*   disfruté – *I enjoyed*

¡qué desastre! – *what a disaster!*   no me gustó – *I didn't like it*

fue emocionante – *it was exciting*   fue increíble – *it was incredible*

¡qué aburrido! – *how boring!*   fue regular – *it was OK*

lo pasé muy mal – *I had an*   lo pasé bomba – *I had a great time*
                     awful time

2 Colour the positive opinions in red. Colour the negative opinions in green.

3 Read this text aloud, adding an opinion in Spanish each time you see ☺ or ☹.

Fui de vacaciones a Cuba ☺. Me alojé en un hotel de lujo ☺. Fui con mi hermano y mis padres ☹. Fuimos a la playa ☺. Bailamos en una discoteca ☺. Viajamos nueve horas en avión ☹.

1 Roll a dice to see what you are going to buy and for whom.

Quiero comprar …	es para …	☺ / ☹
⚀ un vestido de flamenco	⚀ mi hermano	⚀ es muy bonito/a
⚁ una camiseta	⚁ mi madre	⚁ es muy caro/a
⚂ una muñeca	⚂ mi padre	⚂ es muy barato/a
⚃ un abanico	⚃ mi perro	⚃ no gracias, adiós
⚄ una guitarra	⚄ mi profesor	⚄ me gusta
⚅ un sombrero	⚅ mi hermana	⚅ no tengo dinero

2 🎧 Listen to the questions and use your answers from Activity 1 to take part in the conversation.

3 Repeat Activities 1 and 2 until you get to 'no gracias, adiós'.

Recuerdo

The preterite tense is used to say what happened in the past.

1 Draw lines to match up each verb with its infinitive. You must not cross any lines once you have drawn them!

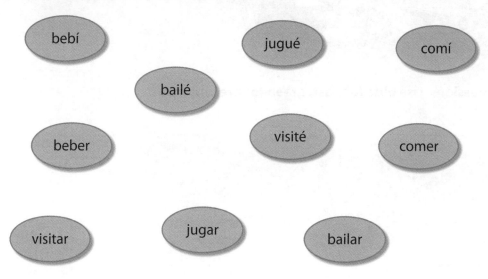

2 Find the Spanish for the following.

a I played _____

b I danced _____

c I visited _____

d I ate _____

e I drank _____

3 Put these sentences into the first person of the past tense.

a Tomar el sol en la playa _____

b Comer en un restaurante _____

c Nadar en el mar _____

d Viajar en avión _____

1 Colour in these time expressions. Use blue for past, green for present and red for future.

> el año pasado
>
> hoy
>
> mañana
>
> ayer
>
> el próximo año
>
> hace dos años
>
> ahora

2 Do the same for these sentences.

   a Fui de vacaciones a España el año pasado.

   b Voy a ir de vacaciones a Francia el próximo año.

   c Normalmente voy de vacaciones a Grecia.

   d Mañana voy a visitar un castillo.

   e Ayer fui a la playa.

3 Write a postcard home. Include two things you did yesterday and three things you are going to do tomorrow.

¿Qué se puede hacer?	What can you do?
se puede	you can / you are allowed
no se puede	you can't / you are not allowed
se puede visitar	you can visit
se puede ir	you can go
se puede ver	you can see
se puede pasear	you can go for a walk
se puede pescar	you can fish
se puede comprar	you can shop / buy
se puede jugar	you can play
se puede hacer	you can do
el río	the river
al aire libre	outdoors / outside
lamentablemente	unfortunately

¿Adónde fuiste?	Where did you go?
el verano pasado	last summer
el invierno pasado	last winter
el año pasado	last year
hace dos años	two years ago
el pasado junio	last June
las Navidades pasadas	last Christmas
hizo sol	it was sunny
hizo calor	it was hot
hizo frío	it was cold
hizo viento	it was windy
hizo buen tiempo	the weather was nice
hizo mal tiempo	the weather was bad
estuvo nublado	it was cloudy
hubo tormenta	there was a storm
hubo niebla	it was foggy
llovió	it rained

¿Qué hiciste?	What did you do?
alojarse / nos alojamos	to stay / we stayed (accommodation)
hacer / hice vela	to do / I did sailing
tomar / tomé el sol	to sunbathe / I sunbathed
bañarse / me bañé en el mar	to swim / I swam in the sea
comer / comimos comida típica	to eat / we ate typical food
relajarse / nos relajamos	to relax / we relaxed
pasear / paseamos	to go for a walk / we went for a walk
sacar / saqué muchas fotos	to take / I took lots of photos
salir / salí de compras	to go out / I went out shopping
comprar / compré recuerdos	to buy / I bought souvenirs
escribir / escribí unas postales	to write / I wrote some postcards
la mayoría de las tardes	most evenings
volver / volví a casa	to return / I returned home

¿Lo pasaste bien?	Did you have a good time?
¡Lo pasé / pasamos fenomenal!	I / we had a great time!
¡Lo pasé / pasamos bomba!	I / we had a blast!

¡Qué aburrido!	How boring!
¡Qué desastre!	What a disaster!
fue / fueron regular	it was / they were average
fue / fueron muy emocionante(s)	it was / they were very exciting
fue / fueron increíble(s)	it was / they were incredible
no estuvo / estuvieron mal	it wasn't / they weren't bad
me / nos encantó	I / we loved it
me / nos gustó	I / we liked it

¿Qué compraste?	What did you buy?
un imán	a magnet
unas castañuelas	castanets
un abanico	a (typically Spanish) fan
una camiseta	a t-shirt
un vestido de flamenco	a flamenco dress
una guitarra española	a Spanish guitar
una muñeca	a doll
un sombrero	a hat
un llavero	a key ring
unas gafas de sol	sunglasses
el/la dependiente	shop assistant
el/la cliente	customer
¿Qué deseas?	What would you like?
¿Cuánto cuesta?	How much does it cost?
muy caro/a	very expensive
algo más barato/a	something cheaper
¡Mira!	Look!
Me lo quedo	I'll take it
¿Algo más?	Anything else?

Checklist

How well do you think you can do the following?			
Write a sentence for each one if you can.			
	I can do this well	I can do this but not very well	I can't do this yet
1. Say what you can do in town			
2. Talk about the weather in the past			
3. Say what you did on holiday			
4. Use the preterite tense			
5. Use time markers			

1 Read and underline the activities and the frequency words.
Then write the correct name under each bar chart.

> Navego por internet de vez en cuando, pero no participo nunca en los chats. Prefiero hablar por teléfono o utilizar correo electrónico. Veo la televisión todos los días, sobre todo los documentales. *David*

> Me encanta ver la televisión. Todos los días veo telenovelas. Me encantan. No tengo ordenador, y no navego nunca por internet. De vez en cuando me gusta escuchar música en la radio, y a menudo leo revistas. *Ana*

> Veo la televisión, pero no mucho. Prefiero jugar con videojuegos. Juego todos los días en internet. Tengo amigos en Australia, Estados Unidos, Inglaterra. Jugamos y a veces chateamos. *Felipe*

> Una vez a la semana leo una revista sobre música. También me gusta navegar por internet a menudo y escuchar música en la radio. No veo nunca la televisión. *Ofelia*

a

b

c

2 Draw the bar chart for the person who is left.

1 **Write out these types of film in order of personal preference.
Start with your favourite.**

☺

las películas románticas   _____

las películas de terror   _____

las películas de ciencia-ficción   _____

las películas de vaqueros   _____

las películas de acción   _____

las películas de misterio   _____

las películas de guerra   _____

las comedias   _____

☹

2 **Use your list to talk about what films you do and don't like.**

me encantan

prefiero

me gustan

no me gustan

odio

no me gustan mucho

3 🎧 **Listen to Alvina and think of a film you would recommend she sees.**

_____

1 🎧 Read the film titles. Then listen. Who saw which film? Write the correct letter.

a Agente Azul y la bomba nuclear

b **En tren para Tombuctú**

c La luna llena: Vampiros en el instituto

d **Amor imposible: Romeo y Julieta**

e Batalla contra el Emperador

1 ☐   4 ☐

2 ☐   5 ☐

3 ☐

2 Read the text and underline these words in Spanish.

I saw   it was   fell in love with   boyfriend   stole   discovered

> Vi una película romántica de ciencia-ficción. Era una comedia.
> Un astronauta se enamoró de una estudiante. El novio de la estudiante, que era vampiro, robó una bomba nuclear.
> El astronauta solucionó el problema cuando descubrió un nuevo planeta.

3 Now translate the whole description into English.

_____

_____

_____

_____

_____

1 **Traffic light the questions:**
Green = I can answer it.
Orange = I understand the question.
Red = I need to revise this.

A Información personal
i   ¿Cómo te llamas?
ii   ¿Cuántos años tienes?
iii ¿Cómo eres?

B Tu vida
i   ¿Qué te gusta hacer en tu tiempo libre?
ii   ¿Cómo es tu rutina diaria?
iii ¿Dónde vives?

C Tus vacaciones
i   ¿Adónde vas de vacaciones?
ii   ¿Qué haces cuando estás de vacaciones?
iii ¿Qué hiciste durante las vacaciones del año pasado?

D Los medios
i   ¿Cómo te comunicas con tus amigos – por móvil, correo electrónico, SMS?
ii   ¿Qué te gusta ver en la televisión?
iii ¿Cuál fue la última película que viste? ¿De qué trató?

2 🎧 **Listen. Which question is each person answering?**

1 _____   4 _____

2 _____   5 _____

3 _____   6 _____

3 **Interview yourself in Spanish using the questions above.**

1 🎧 **Listen and follow the sentences on the grid.**
Sensible (S) or nonsense (N)?

1 S / N

2 S / N

3 S / N

Me encanta	ver	una revista	porque es divertido.
Me gusta	leer	los deberes	porque es aburrido.
No me gusta	hacer	la televisión	porque es emocionante.
Prefiero	hablar con	la radio	porque es educativo.
Odio	escuchar	una hamburguesa	porque es fácil.
Me gustaría	comer	mis amigos	porque es tonto.

2 **Roll a dice and write out the sentence you make. Sensible or nonsense?**

_____

_____

3 **How many sensible sentences can you say in one minute using the grid?**

Recuerdo

To say 'I like it' in Spanish you say 'It pleases me': *Me gusta*.

1 **Think like a Spanish person. Complete the grids.**

Ejemplo:

English	*I like it*
Inbetweenish	*It pleases me*
Spanish	*Me gusta*

English	
Inbetweenish	It pleases him/her
Spanish	Le gusta

English	I like them
Inbetweenish	
Spanish	Me gustan

English	I liked it
Inbetweenish	
Spanish	Me gustó

2 **Decide which grid to use as a model for these sentences. Then translate them into Spanish.**

a I like to watch TV.

_____

b I don't like music.

_____

c He likes to watch TV.

_____

d She likes to talk on the phone.

_____

e I like films.

_____

f I liked the film.

_____

4B.6B Técnica

1 **Complete the grid.**

Verb	Infinitive	Ending	Meaning
come	*comer*	present – he/she/it	*he eats*
bebí		past – I	
habla		present – he/she/it	
jugué		past – I	
fuimos		past – we	
escucho		present – I	

2 **Find the infinitives of these verbs. Look up the meaning of the infinitives in your dictionary.**

salvamos   secuestró   perdieron

_____   _____   _____

rescatan   se casan

_____   _____

3 **Work out what the underlined verbs mean.**

> En la película un gato mágico <u>ayuda</u> a una niña. <u>Buscan</u> a sus padres. <u>Viajan</u> por todo el mundo. <u>Cumplen</u> una serie de aventuras peligrosas. Se <u>reúnen</u> con sus padres.

_____

_____

_____

_____

Los medios y la televisión — *The media and television*

hablo por teléfono	*I talk on the phone*
navego por internet	*I surf the net*
veo la televisión	*I watch TV*
escucho la radio	*I listen to the radio*
juego con videojuegos	*I play computer games*
utilizo el correo electrónico	*I email*
leo los periódicos	*I read the newspapers*
leo revistas	*I read magazines*
participo en los chats	*I use chatrooms*
de vez en cuando	*sometimes*
todos los días	*every day*
una vez / tres veces a la semana	*once / three times a week*
nunca / a menudo	*never / often*
divertido/a	*entertaining*
gracioso/a / tonto/a	*funny / stupid*
emocionante	*exciting*
informativo/a	*informative*
las noticias	*news*
las series	*series*
las telenovelas	*TV soaps*
los anuncios	*adverts*
los concursos	*game shows*
los dibujos animados	*cartoons*
los documentales	*documentaries*
los programas deportivos	*sports programmes*
los programas musicales	*music programmes*

El cine y los libros — *Cinema and books*

una película romántica	*a romantic film*
una película de terror	*a horror film*
una película de ciencia-ficción	*a sci-fi film*
una película de vaqueros	*a cowboy film*
una película de acción	*an action film*
una película de misterio	*a mystery film*
una película de guerra	*a war film*
una comedia	*a comedy*
la fantasía	*fantasy*

¿De qué trató? / ¿Qué pasó? — *What was it about? / What happened?*

un asesinato	*a murder*
un atentado	*a terrorist attack*
un robo	*a robbery*
un secuestro	*a kidnap*
un timo	*a scam*
un viaje	*a journey*
una amistad	*a friendship*
una guerra	*a war*
una historia de amor	*a love story*
una lucha entre el bien y el mal	*a struggle between good and evil*
una misión secreta	*a secret mission*

buscar	*to look for*
batallar	*to fight*
robar	*to rob*
descubrir	*to find*
solucionar	*to solve*
enamorarse de	*to fall in love with*

En mi opinión … — *In my opinion …*

es muy …	*it's very …*
puede ser …	*it can be …*
útil / rápido/a	*useful / quick*
personal	*personal*
educativo/a	*educational*
entretenido/a	*entertaining*
fácil / peligroso/a	*easy / dangerous*
una ventaja es …	*an advantage is …*
una desventaja es …	*a disadvantage is …*
lo malo / bueno es que …	*the bad / good thing is …*
es una pérdida de tiempo	*it's a waste of time*
se puede hacer …	*you can do it …*
con amigos / solo / en casa / donde quieras	*with friends / alone / at home / wherever you like*
se puede llevar consigo / adonde quieras	*you can take it with you / wherever you like*
(no) necesitas tecnología especial	*you (don't) need special technology*
(no) es caro/a	*it's (not) expensive*

Extra — **Extra**

una tontería	*a stupid thing*
tienes que verlo	*you have to see it*
¿No conoces …?	*Don't you know …?*

Checklist

How well do you think you can do the following?

Write a sentence for each one if you can.

	I can do this well	I can do this but not very well	I can't do this yet
1. Talk about types of films and TV programmes			
2. Talk about how you communicate with your friends			
3. Say what happened in a film			
4. Give opinions			
5. Look up verbs in a dictionary			

zoom español 1

Zoom in on your students' needs for KS3 Spanish
with fully integrated video drama

Zoom español is an inspiring two-part Spanish course offering fresh, exciting material and a fully integrated video drama for the whole ability range at Key Stage 3.

The course is flexible and relevant, taking account of the ever increasing diversity of students' abilities and language learning backgrounds. It is fully up-to-date and follows the renewed Key Stage 3 Framework for Languages and the revised Key Stage 3 Programme of Study.

This Workbook provides:

- differentiated practice material for the key language in each unit
- consolidation of key grammar points and language learning skills
- checklists and vocabulary lists for each unit so students can revise the language they've learnt and check their progress
- extra audio material for listening practice

Zoom español Student Book 1	978 0 19 912754 2
Zoom español Foundation Workbook 1	978 0 19 912814 3
Zoom español Higher Workbook 1	978 0 19 912815 0
Zoom español Teacher Book 1	978 0 19 912758 0
Zoom español Audio CDs 1	978 0 19 912757 3
Zoom español Interactive Oxbox 1	978 0 19 912760 3
Zoom español Assessment Oxbox 1	978 0 19 912761 0

OXFORD
UNIVERSITY PRESS

How to get in touch:
web www.oxfordsecondary.co.uk
email schools.enquiries.uk@oup.com
tel 01536 452620
fax 01865 313472

ISBN 978-0-19-912755-9

9 780199 127559